A Cap Fan

by Gavin Hoffman
illustrated by Merrill Rainey

Core Decodable 28

McGraw Hill Education

Bothell, WA • Chicago, IL • Columbus, OH • New York, NY

MHEonline.com

Send all inquiries to:
McGraw-Hill Education
8787 Orion Place
Columbus, OH 43240-4027

ISBN: 978-0-02-144820-3
MHID: 0-02-144820-5

Printed in Canada.

9 10 11 12 KOD 24

Ross has on a Bobcat cap.

Is Ross a Bobcat fan?

Ross is not a big Bobcat fan.

Ross is a big cap fan.

Ross has Pig, Ants, and Frog caps.

Ross has camp and band caps.

Ross stacks stiff caps in glass.

Ross sticks soft caps in a bag.

Not all caps fit Ross.

The black cap was big.
Ross still has it.

Ross can jam on the tan cap.

If a cap rips, Ross still has it.

Got caps? Call Ross!

Ross can pick the caps up.

Ross is a big cap fan!